AF269734

PREDATOR vs. PREY

CROCODILES VS. HIPPOS

FOOD CHAIN FIGHTS

SARAH ROGGIO

Lerner Publications ◆ Minneapolis

Copyright © 2025 by Lerner Publishing Group, Inc.

All rights reserved. International copyright secured. No part of this book may be reproduced, stored in a retrieval system, or transmitted in any form or by any means—electronic, mechanical, photocopying, recording, or otherwise—without the prior written permission of Lerner Publishing Group, Inc., except for the inclusion of brief quotations in an acknowledged review.

Lerner Publications Company
An imprint of Lerner Publishing Group, Inc.
241 First Avenue North
Minneapolis, MN 55401 USA

For reading levels and more information, look up this title at www.lernerbooks.com.

Main body text set in Aptifer Sans LT Pro.
Typeface provided by Linotype AG.

Editor: Cole Nelson **Designer:** Kimberly Morales **Photo Editor:** Nicole Berglund

Library of Congress Cataloging-in-Publication Data

Names: Roggio, Sarah, author.
Title: Crocodiles vs. hippos : food chain fights / Sarah Roggio.
Other titles: Crocodiles versus hippos
Description: Minneapolis : Lerner Publications, [2025] | Series: Predator vs. prey | Includes bibliographical references and index. | Audience: Ages 8–11 | Audience: Grades 4–6 | Summary: "Who rules the Nile, hippos or crocodiles? Readers will enjoy learning about the unique traits of each animal as they explore the ways they attack and defend themselves"— Provided by publisher.
Identifiers: LCCN 2023035219 (print) | LCCN 2023035220 (ebook) | ISBN 9798765626733 (library binding) | ISBN 9798765629369 (paperback) | ISBN 9798765636121 (epub)
Subjects: LCSH: Crocodiles—Juvenile literature. | Hippopotamidae—Juvenile literature. | Predatory animals—Juvenile literature.
Classification: LCC QL666.C925 R65 2025 (print) | LCC QL666.C925 (ebook) | DDC 597.98/2—dc23/eng/20231023

LC record available at https://lccn.loc.gov/2023035219
LC ebook record available at https://lccn.loc.gov/2023035220

Manufactured in the United States of America
2-1012564-52004-4/10/2025

TABLE OF CONTENTS

CHAPTER 1

RUMBLE ON THE NILE RIVER

A MOTHER HIPPO WADES INTO THE NILE RIVER. Her baby swims by her side. The mother hippo dips her head below the surface. But her eyes, ears, and nostrils stay above the waterline. She can still watch and listen for predators. She uses these senses to keep her baby safe.

Hippos use their big jaws to scare away crocodiles.

LOOK OUT! A Nile crocodile swims nearby. The crocodile sinks its body and head below the waterline. But the crocodile can still watch the mother and her baby hippo. The crocodile's eyes, ears, and nostrils are on top of its head.

The mother hippo sees the crocodile dive underwater. She knows it could attack her baby. She opens her huge mouth in a giant yawn. She is warning the crocodile to stay away.

The crocodile decides to make its move. It darts toward the hippos. Its long, strong tail helps it swim fast. Will the crocodile catch its prey?

A Nile crocodile wades into the river to hunt.

HIPPO STATS

AVERAGE WEIGHT: 3,500 to 9,900 pounds (1,588 to 4,491 kg) for males, 3,000 pounds (1,361 kg) for females

BITE STRENGTH: 1,800 pounds per square inch compared to a human bite of 162 pounds per square inch

TOP SPEED: 22 miles (35 km) per hour on land, 5 miles (8 km) per hour in the water

NILE CROCODILE STATS

AVERAGE WEIGHT: 500 to 1,650 pounds (227 to 748 kg) for males, 500 pounds (227 kg) for females

BITE STRENGTH: 5,000 pounds per square inch

TOP SPEED: 18 miles (29 km) per hour on land, 43 miles (69 km) per hour leaping out of the water

Hippos and Nile crocodiles share the same habitat. They both live near the Nile River. The Nile is the longest river on the continent of Africa. In some places, this river overflows onto the land. It forms swamps and lakes where hippos and crocodiles meet. Hippos are huge mammals. Nile crocodiles are reptiles and fierce predators. But are they fierce enough to take on a hippo?

Adult hippos are usually too big to be eaten by a Nile crocodile.

The Nile River flows over 4,000 miles (6,437 km) from below the equator to the Mediterranean Sea.

HIPPOS AND NILE CROCODILES ARE BOTH AGGRESSIVE ANIMALS. They are built to fight. Both have strengths that help them win battles. Which of these two animals rules the Nile? Let's compare their strengths and weaknesses to find out!

DIET AND HUNTING HABITS

Hippos are herbivores. They spend their days in the water and their nights eating grasses and fruit on land. Adult hippos eat over 100 pounds (45 kg) of grass every night!

Nile crocodiles are carnivores. They are often solo and silent hunters. Crocodiles eat large and small prey. They also eat dead animals. They can eat up to half their body weight in one meal. Crocodiles' meals can be as small as a fish or as large as a zebra.

Both hippos and Nile crocodiles can eat a lot of food at one time.

CROCODILE PARENTS

Nile crocodile parents roll their eggs in their mouths to help babies hatch. Mother crocodiles also hide babies in their mouths to keep them away from predators.

SIZE

Hippos are among the largest land mammals on Earth. Male hippos can weigh over 9,900 pounds (4,491 kg). That's twice as much as a truck!

Nile crocodiles can weigh over 1,000 pounds (454 kg). They can grow up to 20 feet (6 m) long. That's over three times the height of an adult man!

Nile crocodiles protect their young. But baby crocodiles usually hunt on their own.

STRENGTH

Hippos have huge mouths, sharp tusks, and long teeth. They open their giant jaws in a wide yawn to scare off predators—and sometimes other hippos.

HIPPOS ARE NAMED AFTER HORSES

Hippo is short for "hippopotamus." This name comes from a Greek word that means "river horse."

Nile crocodiles are built to hunt in the water. They slink through the water to sneak up on their prey. Then they snap their powerful jaws to trap and crush their catch. Crocodiles can also leap up out of the water to catch large animals on land. They drag their prey into the water. Then they drown it before eating it.

CROCODILES LAY DOZENS OF EGGS

Mother Nile crocodiles can lay up to one hundred eggs each mating season. They dig a nest on the shore and cover their eggs with sand to protect them.

Crocodiles are cold-blooded. They need to lie in the sun to keep warm.

Baby hippos can weigh up to 100 pounds (45 kg).

SPEED

Hippos can move quickly despite their big bodies. On land, they can run faster than humans. In water, they can gallop fast enough to catch up to speedboats!

Nile crocodiles are also speedy creatures. They can run as fast as an Olympic athlete on land. They also can sprint out of the water to snatch prey.

HIPPOS DON'T SWEAT

Hippos sometimes look as if they sweat blood, but it's actually an oily, pink liquid. This acts as sunblock for their skin.

AGILITY

Hippos don't swim in the water. In shallow water, they run along the river bottom. In deep water, they leap and jump off the river bottom and close their ears and nostrils to keep the water out.

Hippos often gather in large groups called pods.

Nile crocodiles can hold their breath for over an hour underwater.

Nile crocodiles swim by swishing their tails from side to side. They have flaps that cover their ears and nostrils to keep water out. To move from water to land, crocodiles push forward with their feet and slide on their bellies. On land, they walk on four legs.

MALE NILE CROCODILES MAKE A SPLASH

To attract a female mate, male Nile crocodiles slap their tails and snouts on the water while grunting. Sometimes they also blow water out of their noses.

ATTACK AND DEFENSE STYLES

Hippos are dangerous animals. They mostly fight other hippos to protect their territory. But hippos will also attack other animals—or humans—if they get too close. They have thick skin that protects them from bites.

Hippos fight with their teeth, jaws, and even tails!

A Nile crocodile hunting a pair of zebras

In the water, Nile crocodiles can crush and swallow small animals whole. Near the shore, crocodiles stay below the water. They watch without moving and wait for animals such as zebras to take a drink. Then they leap up on land for a surprise attack. Crocodiles roll their prey underwater to kill it before eating it.

CROCODILES SLEEP WITH ONE EYE OPEN

Unlike humans, Nile crocodiles can shut just one eye while sleeping. They keep the other eye open to watch for predators.

KEY WEAPONS

Hippos' big jaws are their best weapon. They can open their mouths up to 3 feet (1 m) wide. They bite with sharp teeth that grow up to 20 inches (51 cm) long. Their bite is three times stronger than a lion's bite!

Hippos have big, sharp teeth.

MALE HIPPOS MAKE A STINK

Male hippos use their fan-shaped tails to fling poop at other hippos. This helps protect their territory.

Nile crocodiles have one of the strongest bites on Earth. Their powerful jaws help them catch their prey and not let it escape. They have thousands of tiny bumps around their jaws. These bumps help them feel water moving. They can detect even the tiniest movements nearby with their mouths. This helps them find prey in dark water.

WEAKNESSES

Hippos can't breathe underwater. Adult hippos must come up for air every three to five minutes. Baby hippos are born underwater. They swim up to the surface of the water for their first breath. Then they have to come up for air every two to three minutes.

Hippos spend most of their day in the water.

Nile crocodiles have a third eyelid that protects their eyes underwater. But crocodiles can't focus their eyes underwater. This means they can't see clearly. Instead, they rely on sensitive bumps all over their body. These are the same types of bumps they have on their jaws. Crocodiles use these bumps to sense prey and know where to move to catch it.

HIPPOS NAP UNDERWATER

Hippos have a reflex that allows them to bob up to the surface and take a breath without waking up!

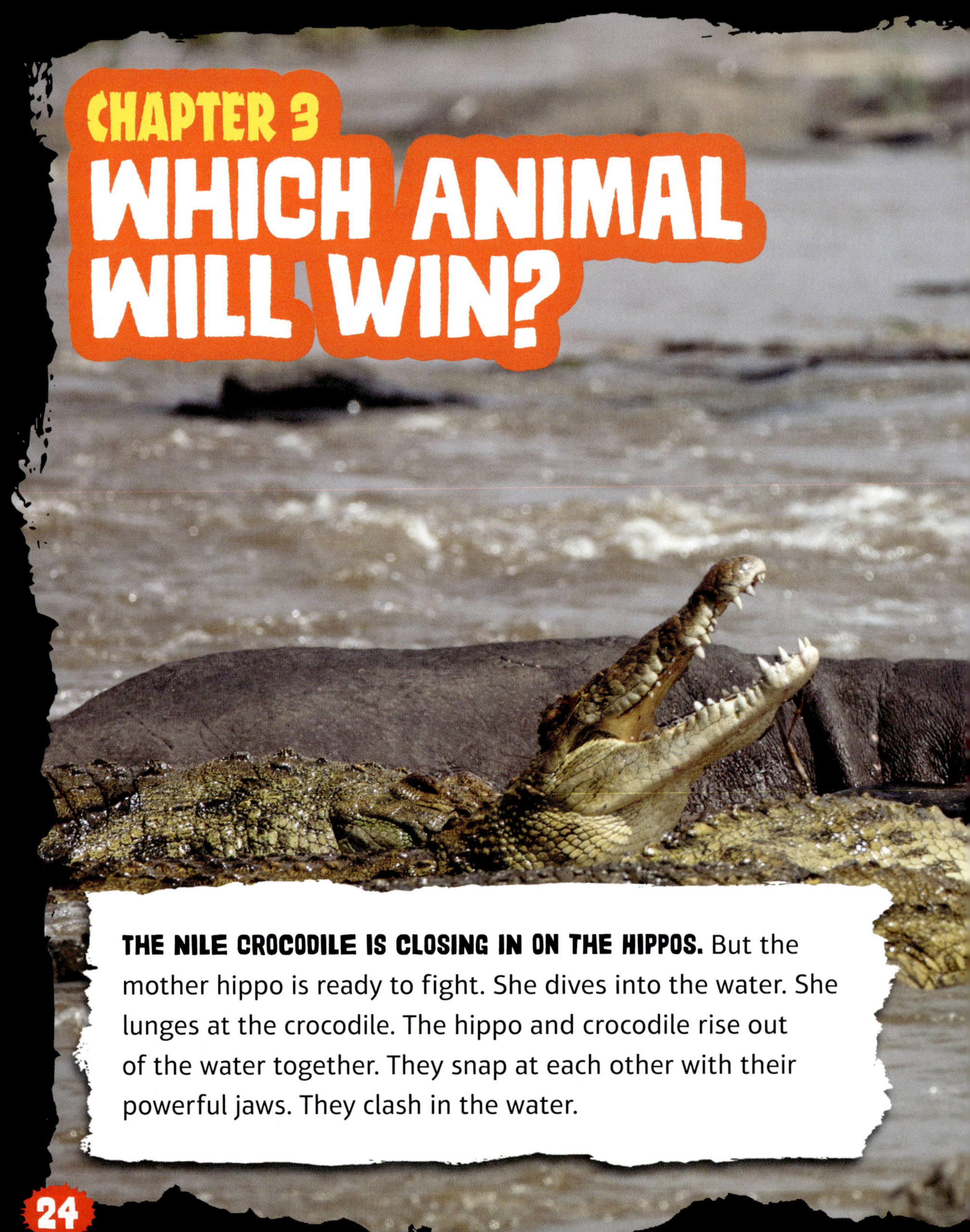

THE NILE CROCODILE IS CLOSING IN ON THE HIPPOS. But the mother hippo is ready to fight. She dives into the water. She lunges at the crocodile. The hippo and crocodile rise out of the water together. They snap at each other with their powerful jaws. They clash in the water.

The crocodile has scales to protect itself. But the crocodile is no match for the mother hippo. She clamps down on the crocodile's bony back. She lifts the crocodile in her powerful jaws. Then she flings it away from her baby. The bruised crocodile swims away. Now that the danger is gone, the mother hippo charges back to her baby. The mother offers her snout as a raft for her tired baby. The baby hippo rests his head. He is safe.

RULER OF THE HABITAT

The Nile crocodile and the hippo are both fierce animals. They keep a close watch on each other in the water. Each animal knows the other can be a dangerous enemy. They can both move fast. They can bite and bruise each other. Crocodiles have bony scales that protect them from hippos. But hippos have one big advantage over crocodiles. Hippos are huge!

Nile crocodiles are hungry, fierce predators!

Most animals—and people—leave hippos alone. After all, an adult hippo can snap a canoe in half with its jaws! Nile crocodiles usually stay away from adult hippos. But a baby hippo is small. That's why the predator crocodile saw the baby hippo as prey.

Today the mother hippo won the battle. The crocodile will need to look somewhere else for its meal. Tomorrow the fight could end differently. But for now, the hippo rules the Nile.

PREDATOR VS. PREY: HEAD-TO-HEAD

HIPPO
- Eyes, ears, and nostrils detect predators.
- A wide yawn is a warning to stay away.

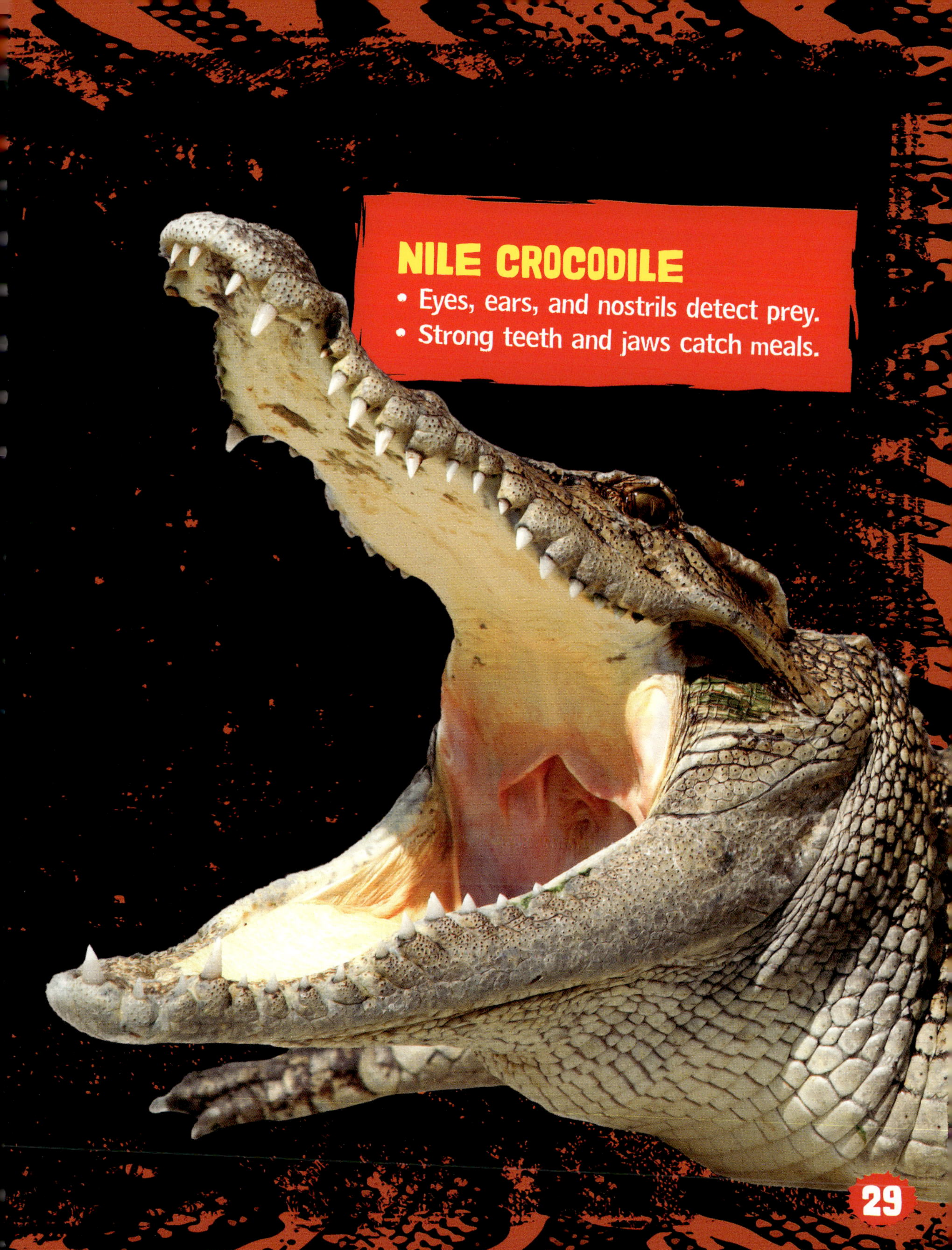

NILE CROCODILE
• Eyes, ears, and nostrils detect prey.
• Strong teeth and jaws catch meals.

GLOSSARY

carnivore: an animal that eats other animals

continent: one of the great divisions of land (as North America, South America, Europe, Asia, Africa, Australia, or Antarctica) on the globe

habitat: the place or type of place where a plant or animal naturally lives or grows

herbivore: an animal that eats plants

mammal: a warm-blooded animal that nourishes its young with milk and has skin usually covered with hair

mate: one in a pair of animals that come together to produce young

predator: an animal that hunts other animals to eat

prey: an animal hunted by another animal for food

reptile: a cold-blooded animal whose babies hatch from eggs

sense: a way that an animal sees, hears, feels, tastes, or smells its surroundings

LEARN MORE

Gillespie, Katie. *Hippo.* New York: AV2, 2022.

Kiddle: Hippopotamus Facts for Kids
https://kids.kiddle.co/Hippopotamus

King, Madeline. *How Strong Is a Crocodile's Bite? World Book Answers Your Questions about Records and Extremes.* Chicago: World Book, 2023.

Markle, Sandra. *On the Hunt with Crocodiles.* Minneapolis: Lerner Publications, 2023.

National Geographic Kids: Hippopotamus
https://kids.nationalgeographic.com/animals/mammals/facts/hippopotamus

National Geographic Kids: Nile Crocodile
https://kids.nationalgeographic.com/animals/reptiles/facts/nile-crocodile

INDEX

PHOTO ACKNOWLEDGMENTS

Image credits: Paul Souders/Getty Images, pp. 4, 5, 19, 24, 25; Michele D'Amico supersky77/Getty Images, p. 6; PhotocechCZ/Shutterstock, pp. 7, 15; Nick Dale/500px/Getty Images, pp. 7, 26; Edwin Godinho/Shutterstock, p. 8; Filippo Maria Bianchi/Getty Images, p. 9; Manoj Shah/Getty Images, pp. 10, 11; Anup Shah/Getty Images, p. 12; Winfried Wisniewski/Getty Images, p. 13; Christian Edelmann/Getty Images, p. 14; Rixipix/Getty Images, p. 16; BirdImages/Getty Images, p. 17; Jupiterimages/Getty Images, p. 18; nattanan726/Getty Images, p. 20; Photopixal/Getty Images, p. 21; Ayzenstayn/Getty Images, p. 22; wolfness72/Shutterstock, p. 23; Jay Bo/Shutterstock, p. 27; Gubin Yury/Shutterstock, p. 28; nattanan726/Shutterstock, p. 29. Design elements: iunewind/Shutterstock; Milano M/Shutterstock; Ukrainian studio/Shutterstock; Cassel/Shutterstock; Textures and backgrounds/Shutterstock; Print Net/Shutterstock.

Cover: pjmalsbury/Getty Images; Jami Tarris/Getty Images.